『고전』 영어로 풀이하기 여덟 번째

천千자字문文 영어 풀이

千	字	文
천	자	문
일천(형용)	글자(명)	글월(명)
thousand	character	text

The Thousand Character Text

천 개의 글자로 이루어진 글월

天	地	玄	黃
천	지	현	황
하늘(명)	땅(명)	검을(형용)	누를(형용)
sky	earth	dark	yellow

The sky is dark and the earth is yellow,

하늘은 검고 땅은 누르며,

김용희 지음

김선생고전영어

천자문 영어 풀이

김용희 지음

지은이
김용희 金容熙

본관은 광산(光山)이며 충남에서 태어났다.
장훈고등학교를 거쳐 경희대학교에서 국제관계학 전공, 법학을 복수전공을 하였다.

주요 저서
《논어 영어로 풀이하다》·《명심보감 영어로 풀이하다》
《사자소학 영어로 풀이하다》·《고사성어 영어로 풀이하다》
《논어 영어로 쉽게 풀이하다》·《천자문 영어로 풀이하다》
《도덕경 영어로 풀이하다》·《천자문 영어 풀이》
《천자문 영어로 풀이하다 E-book》·《사자소학 영어로 풀이하다 E-book》
《천자문 영어로 풀이하다 연습교재》·《사자소학 영어로 풀이하다 연습교재》
《김마스터 영단어 기본편 2000》·《김마스터 영단어 심화편 3600》
《영문법: 천명(God's will)》

천자문 영어 풀이

지음 김용희
표지 디자인 김용희
초판 펴낸 날
단기 4351 년
서기 2018 년
8 월 8 일(양력)

펴낸 곳 김선생 고전영어
경기도 광명시 금당로 11
전화 1668 - 3717
송신 0504-170-0205

∞ 각종 문의 사항은 홈페이지(www.kimmaster.com)로 문의하시기 바랍니다.
∞ 파손된 책은 구매한 곳에서 교환해 드립니다.

천자문 영어 풀이

책을 내놓으며

 천자문이란 책은 한글을 읽을 수 있는 나이의 아이라면 누구 나 "하늘 천(天), 따 지(地), 검을 현(玄), 누를 황(黃)"이라는 말을 들어 봤을 정도로 널리 알려진 책이며, 애니메이션 만화로도 나와 있으니 책에 대한 지명도가 지은이가 지금까지 써 온 6 권의 [고전 영어로 풀이하다]을 더한 것 보다 훨씬 높으리라 생각된다. 그러나 문득 많은 사람 중에 천자문의 첫 번째 글자인 "하늘 천(天)"부터 마지막 글자인 "어조사 야(也)"까지 읽은 사람은 극소수에 불과 할 것이라고 생각되는데 그에 대한 이유는 막상 읽기 시작하면 그 내용이 심오한 부분이 많아 웬만한 배경 지식이 없으면 읽기가 힘들기 때문이다.
 어린 시절 지은이도 천자문에 담긴 내용과 관계 없이 한자의 뜻과 음만 읽고 외우는 것에 치중하였기 때문에 책을 쓰면서 깊은 뜻을 이해하기 위해 생각보다 많은 시간이 걸렸다.
 이것을 교훈 삼아 지은이는 이 책을 쓰면서 독자로 하여금 배경 지식이 없이도 편하게 읽을 수 있도록 하기 위해 많은 노력을 기울였다. 또한 천자문은 본래 1000 자로 이루어진 '1 구(句) 4 자(字)의 사언고시(四言古時) 250 구'로 되어 있으나, 독자의 편의를 위해 기본으로 '한 면에 있는 8 자'를 기준으로 문장을 만들었다. 책을 쓰면서 같은 독자층이 대상인 사자소학과 비교하였을 때 내용과 분량 면에서 천자문이 사자소학보다 더 어렵게 느껴졌으며 독자들도 그러리라 생각된다. 그러한 이유인지 읽고 난 뒤에는 사자소학 보다는 천자문이 더 기쁨을 가져다 준다고 생각한다.

위의 기쁨을 느끼면 지은이는 <<천자문 영어로 풀이하다>> 그리고 <<천자문 영어로 풀이하다 (E-book)>>을 차례로 출간을 하였다.

그러나 두 권의 천자문에 대한 단점을 느꼈는데 <<천자문 영어로 풀이하다>>의 단점은 책의 부피가 커서 가지고 다니기에 불편하다는 것이고 <<천자문 영어로 풀이하다 (E-book)>>은 종이책에서 느낄 수 없는 입체감이 없다는 것이었다.

이에 대해 지은이는 독자들이 가지고 다니면서 입체감을 동시에 느낄 수 있는 <<천자문 영어 풀이>>를 출간을 하였다.

끝으로 단순한 천자문의 음과 뜻을 암기 하기 보다는 시간이 걸려도 자연의 섭리와 중국의 역사를 이해하면서 읽기를 바라며 좋은 문장이 있으면 책에 나온 따라 쓰기 뿐만 아니라 한지(韓紙)에 스스로 붓글씨를 써 보길 바라며 글을 마친다.

The Thousand Character Text (천자문)

 중국 남조 양(502~549)의 주흥사가 양 무제의 명을 받아 지은 책으로, 모두 다른 한자 1000 자로 1 구 4 자의 사언고시 250 구로 되어 있다. 동진 왕희지의 필적에서 해당되는 글자를 모았다고 하는데, 더 오래 전에 중국 위나라 종요의 필적을 모은 것이라는 설도 있고 천자문을 종요가 손수 만들었다는 설도 있다. '천지현황(天地玄黃)'으로 시작해서 '언재호야(焉哉乎也)'의 어조사로 끝나는데, 자연 현상부터 인류 도덕에 이르는 넓은 범위의 글귀를 수록하여 한문의 입문서로 널리 쓰였다.

 당나라부터 빠르게 보급되어 여러 판본이 만들어졌는데, 가장 유명한 것은 왕희지의 7 대손 왕지영이 진서와 초서의 두 서체로 만든 ≪진초천자본(眞草千字本)≫으로 1109 년에 새긴 석각이 남아 있으며 둔황에서 발견된 문서에 그 필사본이 많다고 한다.

 송나라 시대부터는 완전히 정착되어 ≪속(續)천자문≫을 만들기도 하고 ≪서고천자문(敍古千字文)≫과 같이 전혀 다른 글자를 이용한 새로운 천자문이 생기기도 했으며, 천자문의 순서를 이용해 문서 번호를 붙이는 풍습도 생겼다.

 전설에는 주흥사가 무제의 명에 따라 하룻밤 사이에 만들어야 했으나 마지막 4 자를 짓지 못하여 고심하고 있는데, 홀연히 귀신이 나와서 어조사 '언재호야(焉哉乎也)'의 마무리를 알려 주었으며, 완성한 후에 보니 머리털이 하얗게 세었다고 하여 "백수문(白首文)"이라는 별명이 붙었다.

한국(천자문)

≪천자문≫이 한국에 전래된 시기는 명확하지 않다. 일설에 는 일본의 사서 ≪일본서기≫에는 285 년 백제의 왕인(王仁)이 ≪논어≫ 10 권과 함께 ≪천자문≫ 1 권을 일본에 전했다는 기록이 있으므로 백제에는 이보다 훨씬 전에 들어온 것으로 추측하기도 하지만, 이 시기는 천자문의 성립 이전이므로 단순한 전설이라는 것, 일부의 사실을 반영하고 있다는 것, 혹은 또 다른 천자문이라고 하는 것 등의 논란이 있다.

한편, 신라에는 법흥왕 8 년(521 년)에 중국 남조 양의 승려 원표가 사신으로 오면서 많은 불경과 ≪천자문≫을 가지고 왔다고 한다.

천자문은 한문의 입문서로써 줄곧 중용되어 여러 가지 판본이 존재했고 훈민정음 창제 이후 한자마다 그 새김과 소리를 넣어 석음(釋音)을 붙여 간행되었는데, 그 가운데 현존하는 가장 오래된 것은 조선 선조 8 년(1575 년)에 광주(光州)에서 간행된 광주판 천자문이며, 현재 일본 동경대학 중앙도서관에 소장되어 있다.

한국에 가장 널리 보급된 것은 조선시대 선조 16 년(1583 년) 어명에 의해 명필 한호(한석봉)가 쓴 ≪석봉천자문(石峯 千字文)≫으로 여러 차례 중간 되어 왔는데, 현존 하는 여러 판본 중에서 경북 영주의 박찬성(朴贊成) 소장본과 일본 나이카쿠 문고(內閣文庫) 소장본이 원간본 혹은 이것에 가까운 판본으로 추정 된다.

일러 두기

참고 문헌

국내 문헌
- 천자문 (성동호 역해) 홍신문화사
- 한정주 천자문 다산초당
- 주해 천자문 (성백효 편역) 전통문화 연구회
- 한석봉 서체로 천자문 따라 쓰기 천자문 (성명제 역) 효리원
- 한 권으로 끝내는 천자문 (유한나 감수) 지경사
- 천자문 쓰기 교본 (편집부 엮음) 매월당
- 사마천 저 사기 (김원중 역주) 도서출판 민음사

사전
- 시사 엘리트한영사전
- 옥스포드 영한사전
- 민중 활용옥편

위의 것을 제외하고 참고 문헌은 생략하였다.

인칭 대명사의 격변화
일반 명사와는 다르게 대명사는 위치에 따라 모양이 변한다.

주격	목적격	소유격	소유격 대명사
I (나는)	Me (나를, 나에게)	My (나의)	Mine (나의 것)
You (너는)	You (너를, 너에게)	Your (너의)	Yours (너의 것)
He (그는)	Him (그를, 그에게)	His (그의)	His (그의 것)
She (그녀는)	Her (그녀를, 그녀에게)	Her (그녀의)	Hers (그녀의 것)
It (그는)	It (그것을, 그것에게)	Its (그것의)	없음
We (그것은)	Us (우리를, 우리에게)	Our (우리의)	Ours (우리의 것)
They (우리는)	Them (그들을, 그들에게)	Their (그들의)	Theirs (그들의 것)
You (너희들은)	You (너희들을, 너희들에게)	Your (너희들의)	Yours (너희들의 것)

품사 정리

1. 품사
명사(명)
-> [은·는·이·가]를 붙을 수 있는 말이며, 단독으로 의미를 표현할 수 있다.

<u>효도</u>(filial piety)
<u>부모님</u>(parents)
<u>친구</u>(friend)

형용사(형용)
-> 명사를 꾸밀 수 있는 말이다.

<u>좋은</u> 효도(<u>good</u> filial piety)
<u>현명한</u> 부모님(<u>wise</u> parents)
<u>친한</u> 친구(<u>close</u> friend)

동사(동)
-> 행동을 표현하는 말이다.

<u>공부한다</u>(study)
<u>생각한다</u>(think)
<u>사랑한다</u>(eat)

부사(부)
-> 명사 외에 꾸며주는 말이다.

형용사 수식)
<u>진실로</u> 좋은 효도(<u>truly</u> good filial piety)
<u>매우</u> 현명하신 부모님(<u>very</u> wise parents)
동사 수식)
<u>열심히</u> 공부한다(study <u>hard</u>)
부사수식)
<u>정말로</u> 열심히 공부한다(study <u>really</u> hard)

천자문　　　　　　　　　　　　　　　　　　　　　　　영어 풀이

문장 전체수식)
<u>행복하게도</u>, 우리는 한국에 살고 있다.
(<u>Happily</u>, we live in Korea.)

대명사(대명)
-> 앞에 나온 명사를 대신해서 사용하는 말이다.

부모님이 한 소년 보고 있다. <u>그는</u> <u>그분들을</u> 사랑한다.
(Parents see a boy. He loves them)

전치사(전치)
-> 명사 앞에서 장소, 시간, 위치 및 방법을 표현하는 말이다.

장소)
집<u>안에서</u>(in the house)
책상 <u>위에</u>(on the desk)
부모님 <u>옆에</u>(next to parents)

시간)
12 시<u>에</u>(at 12 o'clock)
여름 <u>동안</u>(during summer)

위치)
부모님 옆에서(<u>next to</u> parents)
부모님 앞에서(<u>before</u> parents)

방법)
사랑<u>으로</u>(<u>with</u> love)
걱정 <u>없이</u>(<u>without</u> anxiety)
버스로(<u>by</u> bus)
잉크로(<u>in</u> ink)

접속사(접속)
-> 품사 및 단어 및 문장을 연결해 주는 말이다.

단어 연결)
사랑과 평화(love and peace)
좋고 현명하신 부모님(good and wise parents)

문장 연결)
나는 부모님을 사랑한다 그리고 부모님도 나를 사랑하신다.
(I love parents and they love me too.)

감탄사(감)
-> 느낌표(!)가 붙는 말로 감정을 나타내는 말이다.

슬프구나! (Alas!)

참고-1: 조동사
-> 조동사는 위에서 언급한 8품사 중에 동사에 속하고, 별도의 뜻이 있고 뒤에 반드시 동사 원형이 온다.

should: ~ 해야 한다. (권유)
have to: ~ 해야 한다. (강조)
must: ~ 해야 한다. (강제)
will: ~ 할 것이다.

참고-2: 관사
-> 명사 앞에 놓여 수(數)나 격(格)등을 표현하며 형용사에 속한다.

a·an (부정관사): 하나·같은·종족대표
the (정관사): 하나·바로 그것·종족대표

참고-3: 3인칭 단수 현재형의 동사모습
-> [Be]동사 현재형 am, are, is 중에 is를 쓰는 주어(he·she·it)의 현재형 동사는 무조건 동사의 끝에 s가 붙는다.

am·are -> is
go -> goes
do -> does
have -> has
love ->loves

책 읽는 방법

원문 한자 ->	天	地	玄	黃
원문 발음 ->	천 (품사)	지	현	황
한글 의미 ->	하늘(명)	땅(명)	검을(형용)	누를(형용)
영어 표현 ->	sky	earth	dark	yellow
영문 풀이 ->	The sky is dark and the earth is yellow,			
국문 풀이 ->	하늘은 검고 땅은 누르며,			
	宇	宙	洪	荒
	우	주	홍	황
	집(명)·세계(명)	집(명)·세계(명)	넓을(형용)	거칠(형용)
	house·world	house·sky	wide	rough
	the world is wide and rough.			
	세상은 넓고 거칠다.			

지금까지 배운 한자 수 ------------------------> 8자

천자문(千字文)

본문에 앞서

- 본문 지면에 있는 한자를 스스로 소리 내어 읽기 바랍니다.
- 각 장마다 배운 글자 수가 나와 있으니 참고 바랍니다.
- 어조사가 품사로 쓰이지 않을 때에는 품사를 생략하였습니다.
- 영문 표기는 국립 국어원 로마자 표기법을 적용하였습니다.
- 영문 풀이는 홈페이지에서 무료로 내려 받아 보실 수 있습니다.
- 부록으로 영어 사자소학이 있습니다.
- 한자가 한자 사전에 나와 있는 제일 많이 쓰이는 뜻과 음으로 쓰이지 않을 경우에는 제일 많이 쓰이는 뜻과 음을 천자문에 담긴 뜻과 음과 같이 표기하였습니다.

보기

日
일
날(명)·해(명)
day·sun

본 책의 내용은 지은이의 오랜 노력이 담긴 창작물입니다.
책의 내용을 인용 시 본 책의 출처를 반드시 밝혀주시기 바라며, 위반 시 법에 저촉됨을 알려 드립니다.

天	地	玄	黃
천	지	현	황
하늘(명)	땅(명)	검을(형용)	누를(형용)
sky	earth	dark	yellow

The sky is dark and the earth is yellow,

하늘은 검고 땅은 누르며,

宇	宙	洪	荒
우	주	홍	황
집(명)·세계(명)	집(명)·하늘(명)	넓을(형용)	거칠(형용)
house·world	house·sky	wide	rough

the world is wide and rough.

세상은 넓고 거칠다.

8자

천자문(千字文)

日	月	盈	昃
일	월	영	측
날(명)·해(명)	달(명)	찰(동)	기울(동)
day·sun	moon	fill	go down

If the sun goes down, the moon is filled,

해가 기울면, 달은 가득 차며,

辰	宿	列	張
진	숙·수	열	장
별(명)	잘(동)·별(명)	벌릴(동)	베풀(동)
star	sleep·star	spread	expand

stars spread and expand.

별들은 하늘에 펼쳐져 뻗어 있다.

16자
천자문(千字文)

寒	來	暑	往
한	래	서	왕
찰(명)	올(동)	더울(명)	갈(동)
cold	come	heat	go

If the cold comes, the heat goes,

추위가 오면, 더위가 가며,

秋	收	冬	藏
추	수	동	장
가을(명)	거둘(동)	겨울(명)	감출(동)
autumn	harvest	winter	keep

in autumn, harvest (foods), in winter, keep.

가을에는 수확, 겨울에는 저장한다.

24자

천자문(千字文)

閏	餘	成	歲
윤	여	성	세
윤달(명)	남을(형용)	이룰(동)	해(명)
leap month	extra	make	year

A leap month is made with extra days of a year,

윤달은 일년의 남은 요일로 이루며,

律	呂	調	陽
율	여	조	양
조율(동)	운율(동)·음기(명)	고를(동)	양기(명)
balance	rhythm·Yin	harmonize	Yang

Yin and Yang are balanced and harmonized.

음과 양은 균형과 조화를 이룬다.

32자

천자문(千字文))

雲	騰	致	雨
운	등	치	우
구름(명)	오를(동)	이를(동)	비(명)
cloud	go up	become	rain

If clouds go up, they become rains,

구름은 올라가면 비가 되며,

露	結	爲	霜
로	결	위	상
이슬(명)	맺을(동)	할(동)·변할(동)	서리(명)
dew	form	do·change	frost

formed dew changes into frost.

이슬이 맺어 서리로 변한다.

40자

金	生	麗	水
금	생	여	수
쇠(명)	날(동)	고울(형용)	물(명)
gold	produce	beautiful	water

Yeo-Su (Chinese village) produces gold,

금은 여수(중국의 마을)에서 나고,

玉	出	崑	岡
옥	출	곤	강
구슬(명)	날(동)	메(명)	메(명)
jade	produce	mountain	mountain

Gon-Gang (Chinese mountain) produces jade.

옥은 곤강(중국의 산)에서 난다.

劍	號	巨	闕
검	호	거	궐
칼(명)	이름(명)	클(형용)	대궐(명)
sword	name	big	palace

Geo-gwol is a sword's name,

거궐은 칼 이름이며,

珠	稱	夜	光
주	칭	야	광
구슬(명)	일컬을(동)	밤(명)	빛(명)
bead	call	night	glow

a bead (bright in the night) is called glow.

구슬(밤에 빛나는)은 야광이라 한다.

果	珍	李	柰
과	진	이	내
과실(명)	보배(명)	오얏(명)	능금(명)
fruit	best	plum	apple

plums and apples are the best among fruits,

과일은 오얏(자두)과 능금이 보배며,

菜	重	芥	薑
채	중	개	강
나물(명)	무거울(형용)·중요(형용)	겨자(명)	생강(명)
herb	heavy·important	mustard	ginger

mustards and gingers are important herbs.

나물은 겨자와 생강이 중요하다.

海	鹹	河	淡
해	함	하	담
바다(명)	짤(형용)	강(명)	묽을(형용)
sea	salty	river	fresh

Sea (water) is salty and river is fresh,

바다(물)는 짜고 강(물)은 묽으며,

鱗	潛	羽	翔
린	잠	우	상
비늘(명)	잠길(전치)	깃(명)	날개(명)
scale	under water	feather	wing

fish (scales) are under water, birds (wings) fly.

물고기(비늘)는 물 속에, 새(날개)는 난다.

龍	師	火	帝
용	사	화	제
용(명)	스승(명)	불(명)	임금(명)
dragon	teacher	fire	king

A office with a dragon (B·H) and fire (Y·J),

(복희는)용, (염제는)불로 벼슬을,

鳥	官	人	皇
조	관	인	황
새(명)	벼슬(명)	사람(형용)	황제(명)
bird	office	humanity	emperor

offices with birds (S·H) and (H·W) is humanity.

(소호)새가 벼슬, 황제(헌원)는 어질다.

80자

천자문(千字文)

始	制	文	字
시	제	문	자
처음(부)	만들(동)	글월(명)	글자(명)
first	make	text	letter

First, Chang-hil (Bok-hui's servant) made a letter,

처음에 (창힐이) 글자를 만들고,

乃	服	衣	裳
내	복	의	상
이내(부)·또한(부)	옷(명)	입을(동)	치마(명)
soon·besides	clothes	wear	skirt

besides, were clothes to know status.

또한, 신분구별을 옷을 위해 입어라.

推	位	讓	國
추	위	양	국
밀(동)	자리(명)	양보할(동)	나라(명)
push	state	concede	nation

Je-yo conceded his state to Je-sun,

제요가 제순에게 양보(왕의 자리)하고,

有	虞	陶	唐
유	우	도	당
있을(동)	나라이름(명)	질그릇(명)	당나라(명)
be	Wu	pottery	Tang

Yu-u (J·S) and Do-dang (J·Y) were emperors.

유우(제순)와 도당(제요)은 왕이었다.

弔	民	伐	罪
조	민	벌	죄
조문(동)·불쌍(형용)	백성(명)	벌할(동)	죄(명)
condole·poor	people	punish	fault

Help poor people, punish the faulty,

불쌍한 백성은 돕고, 죄면 벌 주고,

周	發	殷	湯
주	발	은	탕
두루(부)	일어날(동)	은나라(명)	끓을(동)
generally	happen	Eun	boil

Ju-bal, Eun-tang are Ju and Tang king.

주발과 은탕은 주왕과 탕왕이다.

104자

천자문(千字文)

坐	朝	問	道
좌	조	문	도
앉을(동)	아침(명)	물을(동)	길(명)
sit	morning	ask	way

Sitting in the Royal Palace, ask the way,

조정에 앉아 도(길)를 묻고,

垂	拱	平	章
수	공	평	장
드릴(동)	팔짱 낄(동)	평평(형용)·평화(형용)	글(명)·빛날(형용)
drop	fold arms	flat·peaceful	text·bright

dropping and folding arms is peaceful and bright.

손을 내려 팔짱 껴도 평화롭고 밝다.

112자

천자문(千字文)

愛	育	黎	首
애	육	여	수
사랑(명)	기를(동)	검을(형용)	머리(명)
love	raise	black	head

raise people having black hairs with love,

검은 머리 백성을 사랑으로 기르면,

臣	伏	戎	羌
신	복	융	강
신하(명)	엎드릴(동)·복종(동)	오랑캐(명)	오랑캐(명)
servant	lie·obey	barbarian	savage

barbarians (Yung and Gang) obey like servants.

오랑캐(융과 강)도 신하처럼 복종한다.

120자
천자문(千字文)

천자문　　　　　　　　　　　　　　　　　　　　　　　영어 풀이

遐	邇	壹	體
하	이	일	체
멀(형용)	가까울(형용)	한(형용)	몸(명)
far	near	one	body

Countries far and near will be one body,

멀고 가까운 나라가 하나가 되며,

率	賓	歸	王
솔	빈	귀	왕
이끌(동)	손님(명)	돌아갈(동)	임금(명)
lead	guest	come back	king

lead guests, and come back to the king.

그들(손님)을 이끌고 왕에게 돌아가라.

128자

천자문(千字文)

천자문 영어 풀이

鳴	鳳	在	樹
명	봉	재	수
울(동)	봉황(명)	있을(동)	나무(명)
cry	phoenix	be	tree

A phoenix is on the tree, crying,

봉황이 나무 위에서 울며,

白	駒	食	場
백	구	식	장
흰(형용)	망아지(명)	밥(명)	마당(명)
white	colt	meal	ground

white colts eat meal on the ground.

흰 망아지들도 마당에서 밥을 먹는다.

136자

천자문(千字文)

化	被	草	木
화	피	초	목
변할(동)·조화(명)	이불(명)·이를(동)	풀(명)	나무(명)
change·harmony	blanket·spread	grass	tree

Harmony spreads to grass and trees,

조화로움이 풀과 나무에 이르며,

賴	及	萬	方
뢰	급	만	방
신뢰(명)	미칠(동)	일만(형용)	방향(명)
trust	reach	ten thousand	place

trust reaches to all the place.

믿음이 만방(모든 곳)에 이른다.

144자
천자문(千字文)

蓋	此	身	髮
개	차	신	발
덮을(동)	이(대명)	몸(명)	터럭(명)
cover	this	body	hair

Hairs cover this body,

털은 이 몸을 덮고 있으며,

四	大	五	常
사	대	오	상
넉(형용)	큰(명)	다섯(형용)	항상(명)
four	greatness	five	constancy

there are four greatnesses and five constancies.

4개 큰 것과 5개 늘 있는 것이 있다.

恭	惟	鞠	養
공	유	국	양
공손할(형용)	오직(부)	기를(동)	기를(동)
polite	only	raise	raise

Be only polite about raising you,

오직 길러 주심에 공손히 해야하니,

豈	敢	毀	傷
기	감	훼	상
어찌(부)	감히(동)	훼손할(동)	상할(동)
how	dare	injury	hurt

how dare you injury and hurt (your body)?

어찌 감히 (너의 몸) 훼손하느냐?

160자

천자문(千字文)

女	慕	貞	烈
여	모	정	열
계집(명)	사모할(동)	곧을(명)	세찰(부)·굳셀(부)
woman	yearn	courtesy	fiercely·firmly

Women yearn for courtesy firmly,

여자는 곧음을 확고히 바라고(사모),

男	效	才	良
남	효	재	량
사내(명)	본받을(동)	재주(명)	어질(명)
man	follow	skill	good

men follow skill and good.

남자는 재능과 어짊을 본받아라.

知	過	必	改
지	과	필	개
알(동)	허물(명)	반드시(부)	고칠(동)
know	fault	necessarily	correct

If knowing a fault, correct necessarily,

허물을 알면 반드시 고쳐야 하며,

得	能	莫	忘
득	능	막	망
얻을(동)	능할(명)	말(부)	잊을(동)
get	ability	not	forget

if getting ability, don't forget.

능력을 얻으면 잊지 말아야 한다.

176자

천자문(千字文)

罔	談	彼	短
망	담	피	단
없을(부)	말(동)	저(형용)·다른사람(명)	짧을(형용)·단점(명)
not	say	that·others	short·defect

Don't say a defect of others,

다른 사람의 단점을 말하지 말며,

靡	恃	己	長
미	시	기	장
아닐(부)	믿을(동)	몸(명)·자기(명)	길(형용)·장점(명)
not	rely on	body·self	long·merit

don't rely on merit of yourself.

자신의 장점을 믿지 마라.

184자

천자문(千字文)

信	使	可	覆
신	사	가	복
믿을(명)	하여금(동)	가히(부)	덮을(동)·변할(동)
trust	make	well	cover·change

Don't make trust change well,

믿음을 가히 변하게 하지 말며,

器	欲	難	量
기	욕	난	량
그릇(명)	바랄(동)	어려울(형용)	헤아릴(동)
bowl	want	difficult	know

wanting to know a bowl (ability) is difficult.

그릇(능력)은 헤아리기가 어렵다.

192자

천자문(千字文)

墨	悲	絲	染
묵	비	사	염
먹(명)	슬플(형용)	실(명)	물들일(동)
ink	sad	thread	dye

Muk-ja was sad about thread being dyed,

묵(묵자)은 실이 물드는 것을 슬퍼하고,

詩	讚	羔	羊
시	찬	고	양
시(명)	칭찬할(동)	염소(명)	양(명)
poetry	praise	goat	sheep

《Poetry》 praised men in goat clothes.

《시경》은 염소(검소) 옷을 칭찬했다.

200자
천자문(千字文)

景	行	維	賢
경	행	유	현
경치(명)·클(형용)	행할(동)	묶을(동)·근본(명)	현명할(형용)
view·great	do	rope·basis	wise

If doing the great basis, you will be wise,

큰 근본을 행하면 현자가 될 것이며,

克	念	作	聖
극	념	작	성
이길(동)	생각(명)	만들(동)	성인(명)
overcome	thought	make	sage

if overcoming thoughts, you make a sage.

생각(잡념)을 극복하면 성인이 된다.

德	建	名	立
덕	건	명	립
덕(명)	세울(동)	이름(명)	설(동)·세울(동)
virtue	build	name	stand·make

To build virtue is to make your name,

덕을 쌓는 것은 이름을 알리는 것이며,

形	端	表	正
형	단	표	정
모양(명)·얼굴(명)	바를(형용)	겉(명)	바를(형용)
look·face	right	appearance	right

if a face is right, appearance will be right.

얼굴이 바르면 겉도 바르게 된다.

천자문　　　　　　　　　　　　　　　　　　　　　　　영어 풀이

空	谷	傳	聲
공	곡	전	성
빈(형용)	골짜기(명)	전할(동)	소리(명)
empty	valley	spread	sound

An empty valley's sound spreads,

비어 있는 골짜기의 소리는 전달되며,

虛	堂	習	聽
허	당	습	청
빌(형용)	집(명)	익힐(동)	들을(동)
empty	house	practice	hear

empty houses' sound is heard and practiced.

빈 집들의 소리도 들려지고 익혀진다.

224자

천자문(千字文)

禍	因	惡	積
화	인	악	적
불행(명)	인할(동)	악할(명)	쌓을(동)
misfortune	cause	badness	build

To build badness causes misfortune,

악을 쌓는 것은 불행을 일으키며,

福	緣	善	慶
복	연	선	경
복(명)	인연(동)	착할(명)	경사(명)
fortune	cause	goodness	happiness

goodness and happiness cause fortune.

선(착함)과 기쁨(경사)은 복을 부른다.

尺	璧	非	寶
척	벽	비	보
길이(명)·작을(형용)	구슬(명)	아닐(부)	보배(명)
length·small	bead	not	treasure

The length of a bead can't be a treasure,

작은 구슬은 보배가 될 수 없으며,

寸	陰	是	競
촌	음	시	경
마디(명)	그늘(명)	이(대명)	다툴(동)
inch	shade	that	compete

time should be competed (not the bead).

(구슬 말고) 시간(촌음)을 다투어라.

資	父	事	君
자	부	사	군
재물(명)·바탕(동)	아버지(명)	일(명)·섬길(동)	임금(명)
property·base	father	work·serve	king

basing the father, serve the king,

아버지를 바탕으로 임금을 섬기고,

曰	嚴	與	敬
왈	엄	여	경
가로(동)	엄할(부)	더불(접속)	공손할(부)
say	strictly	and	politely

say to them strictly and politely.

그들에게 엄격하고 공손하게 말해라.

248자

천자문(千字文)

孝	當	竭	力
효	당	갈	역
효도(명)	당연히(부)	최선 다할(동)	힘쓸(동)
filial piety	naturally	do one's best	try

Do your best to try filial piety naturally,

당연히 효도의 힘씀에 최선을 다하고,

忠	則	盡	命
충	즉	진	명
충성(명)	곧(부)	다할(동)	목숨(명)
loyalty	that is	devote	life

when in loyalty, that is, devote your life.

충성할 때는, 곧(필요하면), 목숨을 다해라.

256자

천자문(千字文)

臨	深	履	薄
임	심	리	박
임할(동)	깊을(명)	밟을(동)	얇을(명)
face	deep	walk	shallow

On shallows, walk like facing on deeps,

얇은 곳도 깊은 곳을 걷는 것처럼 하며,

夙	興	溫	淸
숙	흥	온	청
일찍(부)	일어날(동)	따뜻할(형용)	서늘할(형용)
early	rise	warm	cool

rise early, and keep (parents) warm and cool.

일찍 일어나, 따뜻하거나 시원한지 봐라.

264자

천자문(千字文)

似	蘭	斯	馨
사	란	사	형
비슷할(전치)	난(명)	그(형용)	향기(명)
like	orchid	that	scent

Like an orchid, keep that scent,

난초와 같이 그 향기롭게 하고,

如	松	之	盛
여	송	지	성
같을(전치)	소나무(명)	어조사	무성할(동)
like	pine	particle	flourish

like a pine, flourish.

소나무와 같이 무성(번창)하라.

272자

천자문(千字文)

川	流	不	息
천	류	불	식
시내(명)	흐를(동)	아니(부)	숨쉴(동)·쉴(동)
stream	run	not	breath·break

A running stream doesn't break,

흐르는 시냇물은 쉬지 않으며,

淵	澄	取	映
연	징	취	영
연못(명)	맑을(형용)	가질(동)	비칠(명)
pond	clean	have	reflection

a clean pond has the reflection.

맑은 연못은 세상을 비춘다.

280자

천자문(千字文)

容	止	若	思
용	지	약	사
얼굴(명)·보일(동)	그칠(동)·거동(동)	같을(전치)	생각(동)
face·show	stop·behave	like	think

Show and behave like thinking,

생각 한 것처럼 행동하고 보여주고,

言	辭	安	定
언	사	안	정
말(명)	말(동)	편안(부)	안정할(부)
word	say	comfortably	easily

say words comfortably and easily.

말은 편안하고 안정되게 하라.

288자

篤	初	誠	美
독	초	성	미
성실할(부)	먼저(부)	정성스러울(부)	아름다울(부) 예의 바를(부)
diligently	first	sincerely	beautiful·mannerly

First, do diligently, sincerely, and mannerly,

먼저, 성실, 정성, 예의 바르게 하며,

愼	終	宜	令
신	종	의	령
신중(부)	마지막(명)	당연할(부)	명령(명)·하여금(동)
carefully	end	naturally	order·make

make an end carefully, naturally,

끝도 당연히 신중하게 하여야 하는데,

296자

천자문(千字文)

榮	業	所	基
영	업	소	기
번성할(동)	업(명)	바(대명)	근본(형용)
develop	work	that	basic

that (289~296) is basic to develop work,

그것(289~296)은 일의 번성에 기본이며,

籍	甚	無	竟
적	심	무	경
문서(명)·이름(명)	심할(부)	없을(전치)	끝날(동)
document·name	well	without	end

(your) name will be well without ending.

이름이 끝없이 널리 남을 것이다.

304자

천자문(千字文)

學	優	登	仕
학	우	등	사
배울(동)	넉넉할(명)	오를(동)	벼슬(명)
learn	much	climb	office

If learning much, you can climb office,

배운 것이 넉넉하면 벼슬에 오르고,

攝	職	從	政
섭	직	종	정
잡을(동)	벼슬(명)	따를(동)·참여할(동)	정사(명)
hold	office	follow	politics

hold office, and follow politics.

벼슬을 잡고, 정치에 참여하라.

存	以	甘	棠
존	이	감	당
있을(동)	로써(전치)	달(형용)	산사나무(명)
be	with	sweet	hawthorn

So-gong was at a sweet hawthorn,

소공은 산사나무에서 있었으며,

去	而	益	詠
거	이	익	영
갈(동)	말이을(접속)	더할(형용)	읊을(동)
leave	but	more	recite

left, but people recited a more poem for him.

그가 떠나가도 그를 위해 시를 읊었다.

樂	殊	貴	賤
악	수	귀	천
풍류(명)	다를(부)	귀할(명)	천할(명)
elegance	differently	high	low

The elegance has high and low differently,

풍류에도 귀천이 다르게 있으며,

禮	別	尊	卑
예	별	존	비
예절(명)	분별(동)	높을(명)	낮을(명)
manners	distinguish	upper	lower

manners distinguishes the upper from lower.

예절은 윗사람과 아랫사람을 분별한다.

上	和	下	睦
상	화	하	목
위(명)	화목할(형용)	아래(명)	화목할(형용)
senior	peaceful	junior	peaceful

If a senior is peaceful, a junior is peaceful,

윗사람이 화목하면 아랫사람도 화목하고,

夫	唱	婦	隨
부	창	부	수
남편(명)	노래(명)·이끌(동)	아내(명)	따를(동)
husband	song·guide	wife	follow

if a husband guides, a wife follows.

남편이 이끌면 부인은 따른다.

336자

천자문(千字文)

外	受	傅	訓
외	수	부	훈
바깥(명)	받을(동)	스승(명)	가르침(명)
outside	receive	teacher	lesson

In outside, receive a lesson from a teacher,

밖에서는 스승의 가르침을 받으며,

入	奉	母	儀
입	봉	모	의
들(동)	받들(동)	어미(명)	행동(명)
come	follow	mother	behavior

if coming, follow mother's behavior.

들어오면 어머니의 행실을 본받는다.

諸	姑	伯	叔
제	고	백	숙
모두(형용)	고모(명)	큰삼촌(명)	작은삼촌(명)
all	aunt	elder uncle	younger uncle

All aunt, elder uncle, and younger uncle should

고모, 백부(큰), 숙부(작은) 모두는

猶	子	比	兒
유	자	비	아
같을(전치)	아들(명)	비교(동)	아이(명)
as	child	think of	kid

think of other kids as their children.

다른 아이도 자기 자식으로 비교해라.

孔	懷	兄	第
공	회	형	제
구멍(명)·매우(부)	품을(동)	맏(명)	아우(명)
hole·well	get along	elder brother	little brother

Brothers should get along well,

형제는 매우 사이 좋게 지내야 함은,

同	氣	連	枝
동	기	연	지
같을(형용)	기운(명)	이을(동)	가지(명)
same	spirit	stem	branch

as they stem from the same branch and spirit.

같은 가지와 기운에서 나왔기 때문이다.

360자

천자문(千字文)

交	友	投	分
교	우	투	분
사귈(동)	벗(명)	던질(동)·줄(동)	나눌(명)·신분(명)
associate	friend	throw·give	share·status

Associate with friends giving the status,

신분에 맞는 친구를 사귀고,

切	磨	箴	規
절	마	잠	규
끊을(동)·절실할(부)	갈(동)·연마할(동)	경계(부)	법(명)·도리(명)
cut·earnestly	grind·practice	carefully	law·justice

practice justice earnestly and carefully.

도리를 절실히 주의 깊게 닦아라.

仁	慈	隱	惻
인	자	은	측
어질(명)	자비(명)	숨을(동)·가여운(명)	측은(명)
virtue	mercy	hide·compassion	pity

Virtue, mercy, compassion, and pity

어짊, 자비, 가여운 마음, 측은함은

造	次	弗	離
조	차	불	리
지을(동)	버금(형용)	아닐(부)	떠날(동)
make	next	not	leave

don't leave for even a moment.

짧은 시간(조차)도 떨어져서는 안 된다.

節	義	廉	退
절	의	염	퇴
마디(명)·절개(명)	정의(명)	청렴(명)	물러날(명)
joint·fidelity	justice	integrity	retreat

Fidelity, justice, integrity, and retreat

절개, 정의, 청렴 그리고 물러남은

顚	沛	匪	虧
전	패	비	휴
기울어질(동)	넘어질(동)	아닐(부)	약해질(동)
collapse	fall	not	weaken

don't weaken, if collapsing and falling.

넘어지고 쓰러져도 약해지면 안 된다.

384자

천자문(千字文)

性	靜	情	逸
성	정	정	일
성품(명)	고요할(형용)	감정(명)	편안할(형용)
nature	calm	feeling	comfortable

If nature is calm, feeling is comfortable,

성품이 조용하면 감정도 편안하고,

心	動	神	疲
심	동	신	피
마음(명)	움직일(동)	정신(명)	피곤할(형용)
mind	shake	spirit	fatigue

if mind shakes, spirit is fatigue.

마음이 흔들리면 정신이 피곤하다.

392자
천자문(千字文)

守	眞	志	滿
수	진	지	만
지킬(동)	참(명)	뜻(명)	가득(동)
keep	truth	will	fill

If keeping the truth, the will is filled,

진실을 지키면 뜻이 가득 차고,

逐	物	意	移
축	물	의	이
쫓을(동)	물건(명)·재물(명)	뜻(명)	옮길(동)
pursue	thing·property	meaning	change

if pursuing property, meaning changes.

재물을 쫓으면 좋은 뜻이 변한다.

堅	持	雅	操
견	지	아	조
굳을(부)	가질(동)	우아할(형용)·바를(형용)	잡을(동)·지조(명)
firmly	have	elegant·right	hold·principle

If having the right principle firmly,

바른 지조를 굳게 가지고 있으면,

好	爵	自	縻
호	작	자	미
좋을(형용)	벼슬(명)	스스로(부)	생길(동)
likable	office	naturally	happen

likable office happens naturally.

좋은 벼슬이 스스로 생겨난다.

都	邑	華	夏
도	읍	화	하
도시(명)	고을(명)	빛날(형용)	여름(명)
town	village	bright	summer

Hwa-ha (China) made towns and villages,

화하(중국)가 도읍(큰 도시)을 정하니,

東	西	二	京
동	서	이	경
동녘(명)	서녘(명)	두(형용)	서울(명)
east	west	two	capital

in the east and west are two capitals.

동쪽과 서쪽에 두 개의 서울이 있다.

416자

천자문(千字文)

背	芒	面	洛
배	망	면	락
등(명)	산 이름(명)	낯(명)·앞(명)	낙수(명)
back	mountain	front	water

Mt. Buk is at back, Nak water is at front,

뒤에는 북망산이 앞에는 낙수가 있고,

浮	渭	據	涇
부	위	거	경
뜰(동)·흐를(동)	물 이름(명)	근거할(동)	물 이름(명)
float	water	ground	water

Wi water floats and base on Gyeong water.

위수가 흐르며 경수를 근거로 한다.

424자

천자문(千字文)

宮	殿	盤	鬱
궁	전	반	울
집(명)	궁궐(명)	소반(명)	우거질(형용)
house	palace	tray	many

As there are many palaces,

많은 궁전들이 있어서,

樓	觀	飛	驚
루	관	비	경
누각(명)	볼(동)	날(동)	놀랄(동)
upstairs	look at	fly	surprise

on upstairs, if looking at, you fly, surprised.

2층(누각)에서 보면 놀라서 날 것이다.

圖	寫	禽	獸
도	사	금	수
그림(명)	그릴(동)	날짐승(명)	들짐승(명)
painting	draw	bird	animal

Drawing birds and animals in a painting,

새들과 짐승들의 그림을 그리며,

畫	彩	仙	靈
화	채	선	령
그림(명)	무늬(명)·채색(동)	신선(명)	신령(명)
painting	pattern·color	hermit	spirit

color hermits and spirits in the painting.

신선과 신령들을 그림에 색칠 하였다.

丙	舍	傍	啓
병	사	방	계
남녘(명)	집(명)	곁(전치)	일깨울(동)·열(동)
south	building	next to	enlighten·open

Next to Byeong-sa (building), open the door,

병사(건물)를 곁에 두고 문을 열고,

甲	帳	對	楹
갑	장	대	영
갑옷(명)	휘장(명)	대답할(동)·마주할(동)	기둥(명)
armor	curtain	reply·sit opposite	pillar

Gap-jang (colorful curtains) sits opposite pillars.

갑장(화려한 휘장)이 기둥 사이에 마주한다.

肆	筵	設	席
사	연	설	석
늘어놓을(동)	자리(명)	베풀(동)·만들(동)	자리(명)
place	mat	make	seat

Placing a mat and making a seat,

자리를 늘어놓으며 좌석을 만들고,

鼓	瑟	吹	笙
고	슬	취	생
북(명)·두들길(동)	비파(명)	불(동)	생황(명)
drum	harp	blow·play	flute

drum the harp and play the flute.

비파를 치고 생황을 분다.

456자

천자문(千字文)

陞	階	納	陛
승	계	납	폐
오를(동)	계단(명)	들일(동)	섬돌(명)
go up	stair	enter	stone step

Going up stairs, enter stone steps,

계단에 올라 섬돌로 들어가니,

弁	轉	疑	星
변	전	의	성
고깔(명)	옮길(동)·움직일(동)	의심할(동)	별(명)
hat	wave	doubt	star

hats (ornaments) waving, doubt stars.

모자(장식물)들이 움직여 별인가 의심스럽다.

右	通	廣	內
우	통	광	내
오른쪽(명)	통할(동)	넓을(형용)	안(형용)
right	pass	wide	inner

On the right, pass Gwang-nae (building),

오른쪽은 광내(건물)가 지나가고,

左	達	承	明
좌	달	승	명
왼(명)	통달할(동)	이을(동)	밝을(형용)
left	pass	succeed	bright

on the left, pass Seung-myeong (building).

왼쪽은 승명(건물)으로 지나간다.

472자

천자문(千字文)

旣	集	墳	典
기	집	분	전
미리(부)	모을(동)	무덤(명)	법(명)
ahead	collect	grave	law

Collect, ahead, Bun (book) and Jeon (book),

미리 분(책)과 전(책)을 모여 있고,

亦	聚	群	英
역	취	군	영
또(부)	모을(동)	무리(형용)·많은(형용)	인재(명)
also	gather	many	talent

also, gather many talents.

또한 많은 인재들도 모여 있다.

480자

천자문(千字文)

杜	藁	鍾	隷
두	고	종	례
막을(동)	짚(명)	쇠북(명)	글씨(명)
protect	straw	drum	text

Du-do's grass characters, Jong-yo's angular styles,

두도(사람)의 초서와 종요(사람)의 예서,

漆	書	壁	經
칠	서	벽	경
옷 칠(동)	책(명)	벽(명)	경전(명)
lacquer	book	wall	bible

lacquered books and bibles are in the wall.

벽 속에 옷 칠로 된 책과 경전들이 있다.

府	羅	將	相
부	라	장	상
관청(명)	늘어설(동)	장수(명)	서로(부)
office	stand	general	together

In the office, generals stand together,

관청에는 장수들이 서로 늘어서고,

路	挾	槐	卿
로	협	괴	경
길(명)	낄(동)·같이(부)	회화나무(명)·삼공(명)	벼슬(명)
road	fold·together	sophora·three dukes	officer

three dukes and officers are on the road together.

길에는 삼공(벼슬)들과 경(벼슬)들이 있다.

496자

천자문(千字文)

戶	封	八	縣
호	봉	팔	현
문(명)·집(명)	봉할(동)·줄(동)	여덟(형용)	고을(명)
door·house	seal·give	eight	county

As a house, Han state gave eight counties,

한(漢)나라는 구역(집)으로 여덟 고을을 주고,

家	給	千	兵
가	급	천	병
집(명)	줄(동)	일천(형용)	병사(명)
house	give	thousand	solider

gave a thousand soldiers to the house.

집에 천 명의 병사를 주었다.

高	冠	陪	輦
고	관	배	련
높을(형용)	갓(명)	모실(동)	수레(명)
high	hat	serve	wagon

High hats (high officer) serve a wagon,

높은 갓(높은 벼슬의 사람)이 수레를 몰고,

驅	轂	振	纓
구	곡	진	영
몰(동)	바퀴(명)	떨친(동)·흔들릴(동)	갓끈(명)
turn	wheel	swing·wave	hat string

turning wheels, hat strings wave.

바퀴가 구를 때 갓끈이 흔들린다.

世	祿	侈	富
세	록	치	부
세대(명)	녹봉(명)	사치(명)	부유할(명)
generation	pay	luxury	wealth

For the generation, with pay, luxury, wealth,

녹을 받는 대대로 사치와 부가 있고,

車	駕	肥	輕
거	가	비	경
수레(명)	탈것(명)	살찔(명)	가벼울(형용)
wagon	vehicle	fat	light

fat (horse) draw light wagons and vehicles.

살찐 것(말)이 가벼운 수레를 끈다.

策	功	茂	實
책	공	무	실
계획할(동)	공로(명)	무성할(동)	실적(명)
plan	merit	increase	result

Planning merits and increasing results,

공로를 계획하고 실적을 많이 쌓으며,

勒	碑	刻	銘
늑	비	각	명
새길(동)	비석(명)	새길(동)	이름 새길(동)
engrave	tombstone	engrave	engrave a name

engrave a name on a tombstone.

비석에 이름을 새긴다.

528자

천자문(千字文)

潘	溪	伊	尹
반	계	이	윤
물가(명)	시내(명)	저(형용)	다스릴(동)
water	stream	that	govern

Ban-gye (Gang-tae-gong) and I-yun (A-hyeong)

반계(강태공)와 이윤(아형)은

佐	時	阿	衡
좌	시	아	형
도울(동)	때(명)	언덕(명)	저울(명)
help	time	slope	scale

are helpers (found of Ju and Eun state).

도운 사람들이다(주나라와 은나라).

奄	宅	曲	阜
엄	택	곡	부
덮을(동)·다스릴(동)	집(명)	굽을(동)	언덕(명)
cover	house	curve	slope

Cover Gok-bu (area)'s house,

곡부의 집(땅)을 다스리니,

微	旦	孰	營
미	단	숙	영
세심할(부)	아침(명)	누구(명)	경영(동)
in detail	morning	who	manage

who manages it in detail? Dan (Ju-gong).

누가 세심히 다스리냐? 단(주공)만이 한다.

544자

천자문(千字文)

桓	公	匡	合
환	공	광	합
굳셀(형용)	벼슬(명)	바를(부)	화합(동)
strong	duke	uprightly	unify

Hwan duke unified uprightly,

(제)환공은 천하를 바르게 화합하고,

濟	弱	扶	傾
제	약	부	경
구제할(동)	약할(형용)	도울(동)	기울어질(명)
relieve	weak	help	decline

relieved the weak, and helped the decline (state).

약자를 구제하고 기우는 나라를 도왔다.

552자
천자문(千字文)

綺	回	漢	惠
기	회	한	혜
비단(명)	돌이킬(동)·되찾을(동)	한나라(명)	은혜(명)
silk	return·replace	Han state	bless

Gi-ri-gye replaced Hye-je of Han state,

기(기리계)가 한 혜(혜제)의 자리를 되찾아 주고,

說	感	武	丁
열	감	무	정
말씀(명)·기쁠(형용)	감동(동)	호반(명)	고무래(명)
word·glad	impress	military	rake

Bu-yeol impressed Mu-jeong (King of Sang state).

열(부열)은 무정(상나라 왕)을 감동시켰다.

俊	乂	密	勿
준	예	밀	물
뛰어날(명)	어질(명)	밀집(형용)·높은(형용)	말(동)·물론(부)
good	virtue	dense·high	do not·surely

Surely, the high good and virtue,

물론, 높은 뛰어남과 어짊,

多	士	寔	寧
다	사	식	녕
많을(형용)	선비(명)	이(대명)	편안할(형용)
many	scholar	this	peaceful

many scholars, this is peaceful.

많은 선비들, 이것이 평화이구나.

568자

천자문(千字文)

晉	楚	更	霸
진	초	경	패
진나라(명)	초나라(명)	고칠(동)·바꿀(동)	우두머리(명)
Jin state	Cho state	repair·change	chief

Jin (Mun duke), Cho (Jang king) changed a chief,

진(문공)과 초(장왕)가 바뀌며 패자가 되고,

趙	魏	困	橫
조	위	곤	횡
조나라(명)	위나라(명)	곤할(명)	가로(부)
Jo state	Wi state	difficulty	crosswise

Jo and Wi had difficulty for Heong (strategy).

조와 위나라는 횡(전술)때문에 곤란하였다.

假	途	滅	虢
가	도	멸	괵
빌릴(동)	길(명)	멸할(동)	나라이름(명)
rent	way	ruin	Goek

After renting a way from Goek, to ruin Goek,

길을 빌려 곽나라를 멸하고,

踐	土	會	盟
천	토	회	맹
밟을(동)	흙(명)	모일(동)	맹세할(동)
step	earth	gather	swear

gathering in Cheon-to (place), to swear.

천토(장소)에 모여 맹세를 하였다.

何	遵	約	法
하	준	약	법
어찌(부)	따를(동)	대략(부)·간략할(형용)	법(명)
how	follow	about·simple	law

So-ha followed the simple law,

하(소하)는 간략한 법을 따르고,

韓	弊	煩	刑
한	폐	번	형
한나라(명)	곤란(명)	복잡할(형용)	형벌(명)
Han state	hardship	complex	law

Han-bi-ja had hardship for the complex law.

한(한비자)은 복잡한 형법 때문에 곤란을 겪었다.

592자

천자문(千字文)

起	翦	頗	牧
기	전	파	목
일어날(동)	가위(명)	치우칠(명)	기를(동)
awake	scissor	unbalance	raise

Baek-gi, Wang-jeon, Yeom-pa, and I-mok

기(백기), 전(왕전), 파(염파), 그리고 목(이목)은

用	軍	最	精
용	군	최	정
쓸(동)·다룰(동)	군사(명)	최고(부)	정할(부)
use	soldier	extremely	finely

used soldiers extremely and finely,

군사를 최고로 훌륭히 잘 다루었고,

宣	威	沙	漠
선	위	사	막
베풀(동)·알릴(동)	위엄(명)	모래(명)	넓을(형용)
give·spread	dignity	sand	wide

spread dignity to the desert,

사막까지 위엄을 알렸으며,

馳	譽	丹	靑
치	예	단	청
달릴(동)·남길(동)	명예(명)	붉을(형용)	푸를(형용)
run	honor	red	blue

honor ran with Dan-cheong (picture).

단청(그림)으로 명예를 남겼다.

천자문　　　　　　　　　　　　　　　　　　　　영어 풀이

九	州	禹	跡
구	주	우	적
아홉(형용)	고을(명)	우임금(명)	흔적(명)
Nine	village	King U	trace

Nine villages are King U's trace,

아홉 개의 고을들은 우임금의 흔적이고,

百	郡	秦	竝
백	군	진	병
일백(형용)	고을(명)	나라 이름(명)	아우를(동)
hundred	district	Jin state	manage

Jin state managed one-hundred districts.

일백 개의 고을은 진나라가 다스린다(아우름).

616자
천자문(千字文)

嶽	宗	恒	岱
악	종	항	대
큰 산(명)	으뜸(형용)	항상(부)	터(명)
big mountain	best	always	place

Hang and Dae are best big mountains,

항산과 대산은 으뜸인 큰 산들이며,

禪	主	云	亭
선	주	운	정
신선(명)	주인(명)	이를(동)	정자(명)
hermit	main	call	arbor

Un and Jeong are mains of a hermit (rite).

운과 정은 신선(봉선제)의 주된 곳이다.

624자
천자문(千字文)

천자문 영어 풀이

鴈	門	紫	塞
안	문	자	새
기러기(명)	문(명)	붉을(명)	변방(명)
wild goose	door	purple	frontier

An-mun, Ja-sae,

안문, 자새,

鷄	田	赤	城
계	전	적	성
닭(명)	밭(명)	붉을(형용)	성(명)
chicken	field	red	castle

Gye-jeon, Jeok-seong (place),

계전, 적성,

昆	池	碣	石
곤	지	갈	석
맏(명)	연못(명)	비석(명)	돌(명)
eldest	lake	tombstone	stone

Gon-ji (lake), Gal-seok (mountain),

곤지(호수), 갈석(산),

鉅	野	洞	庭
거	야	동	정
클(형용)	들(명)	고을(명)	뜰(명)
big	field	village	garden

Geo-ya (swamp), Dong-jeong (lake)

거야(늪), 동정(호수)들이,

曠	遠	綿	邈
광	원	면	막
멀(명)	멀(부)	솜(명)·이어질(동)	멀(부)
distance	far	cotton·connect	away

connect in the distance and far away,

멀고 멀리 이어져 있고,

巖	岫	杳	冥
암	수	묘	명
바위(명)	산봉우리(명)	아득할(부)	어두울(형용) 그윽할(부)
rock	mountain peak	away	dark·subtly

rocks and mountain peaks are away and subtly.

바위와 산봉우리도 아득하고 그윽이 있다.

천자문 영어 풀이

治	本	於	農
치	본	어	농
다스릴(동)	기본(부)	어조사(전치)	농사(명)
govern	basically	with	agriculture

Basically, govern with agriculture,

기본으로 농사로 다스리고,

務	茲	稼	穡
무	자	가	색
힘쓸(동)	이(형용)·더욱(부)	심을(동)	거둘(동)
try	this·further	plant	harvest

further, try to plant and harvest.

심고 거두는 것에 더욱 힘써야 한다.

656자

천자문(千字文)

俶	載	南	畝
숙	재	남	묘
드디어(부)	실을(동)	남녘(명)	이랑(명)
finally	fill	south	furrow

Finally, fill furrows in the south,

드디어 남쪽 이랑(밭)을 채우고,

我	藝	黍	稷
아	예	서	직
나(명)	재주(명)·심을(동)	기장(명)	피(명)
I	talent·plant	millet	grass

I plant millet and grass.

나는 기장과 피를 심는 재주가 있네.

664자

천자문(千字文)

稅	熟	貢	新
세	숙	공	신
세금(동)	익을(형용)	바칠(동)	새로울(형용)
tax	ripe	offer	new

Tax the ripe, offer the new,

익은 곡식엔 세금을, 새것은 공물로 바치며,

勸	賞	黜	陟
권	상	출	척
권할(동)	상줄(동)	내칠(동)	오를(동)
advise	prize	send	promote

advise, prize, send, and promote it.

권하고, 상 주고, 내치고, 그리고 올려준다.

孟	軻	敦	素
맹	가	돈	소
맏(명)	수레(명)	돈독할(동)	바탕(명)
elder brother	cart	strengthen	basis

Maeng-ga (Maeng-ja) strengthened basis,

맹가(맹자)는 바탕을 돈독히 하였고,

史	魚	秉	直
사	어	병	직
역사(명)	물고기(명)	가질(동)	곧을(명)
history	fish	have	honesty

Sa-eo (a minister of Wi state) had honesty.

사어(위나라 재상)는 곧음을 가지고 있었다.

庶	幾	中	庸
서	기	중	용
무리(명)·가까울(동)	몇(형용)·가까울(동)	가운데(명)	떳떳할(형용)
many·approach	some·approach	middle	honorable

To approach Jung-Yong (the golden mean),

중용에 가까워지기 위해서는,

勞	謙	謹	勅
로	겸	근	칙
노력(동)	겸손할(형용)	삼가할(형용) 신중할(형용)	칙서(명)·경계할(형용)
work hard	modest	cautious	edict·alert

work hard, be modest, cautious, and alert.

노력, 겸손, 신중하고, 그리고 경계하라.

聆	音	察	理
영	음	찰	리
들을(동)	소리(명)	살필(동)	이치(명)
hear	sound	observe	reason

hearing the sound, observe the reason,

소리를 듣고 이치를 살피고,

鑑	貌	辨	色
감	모	변	색
볼(동)	모양(동)	분별(동)	빛(명)·낯(명)
see	appearance	recognize	color·face

seeing appearance, recognize the face.

겉을 보면, 낯(상황)을 분별해야 한다.

貽	厥	嘉	猷
이	궐	가	유
줄(동)	그(형용-)	아름다울(형용) 좋을(형용)	계획(명)
hand down	the	beautiful·good	plan

Hand down the good plan,

좋은 계획을 전해주고,

勉	其	祗	植
면	기	지	식
노력할(동)	그(대명)	공경(부)	심을(동)
try	it	politely	keep

try to keep it politely.

공경하게 그것을 간직(심는)하는 것에 노력해라.

704자

천자문(千字文)

省	躬	譏	誡
성	궁	기	계
살필(동)	몸(명)	나무랄(동)·성찰할(동)	경계할(동)
observe	body	scold·reflect	watch out

Observe, reflect, and watch out for your body,

몸을 살피고, 성찰하고, 그리고 경계하고,

寵	增	抗	極
총	증	항	극
총애(명)	더할(동)	다툴(동)	다할(동)·끝(명)
favor	gain	dispute	end

if gaining favor, dispute the end.

총애를 얻으면, 끝을 조심(다툼)해라.

殆	辱	近	恥
태	욕	근	치
위험할(형용)	욕될(명)	가까울(형용)	부끄러움(명)
dangerous	dishonor	close	disgrace

If dishonor is danger and close to disgrace,

욕됨이 위험하고 부끄럼에 가까우면,

林	皐	幸	卽
임	고	행	즉
수풀(명)	언덕(명)	행복(형용)	곧(부)
forest	hill	happy	soon

soon, in the forest and hill, be happy.

곧(즉시), 숲과 언덕에서 행복해라.

兩	疏	見	機
양	소	견	기
두(형용)	소통(동)	볼(동)	틀(명)
two	communicate	see	condition

As two So (So-gwang and So-su) saw a condition,

양소(소광과 소수)는 상황(틀)을 보고,

解	組	誰	逼
해	조	수	핍
풀(동)	끈(명)	누구(명)	핍박(동)
untie	string	who	pressure

they untied strings, who pressured them?

끈을 푸니(관직을 버림)니, 누가 핍박하리요?

728자

천자문(千字文)

索	居	閑	處
색	거	한	처
찾을(동)	살(동)	한가(형용)	곳(명)
search	live	free	place

Search the free place, and live,

한가한 곳을 찾고 그곳에 살아라,

沈	默	寂	寥
침	묵	적	요
가라앉을(동)	잠잠할(부)	고요할(부)	한적할(부)
sink	silently	quietly	solitarily

sinking, silently, quietly, and solitarily.

은둔하면서, 조용히, 고요히, 그리고 한적하게.

736자

천자문(千字文)

求	古	尋	論
구	고	심	론
구할(동)	옛(명)	찾을(동)	논의(동)
pursue	past	search	discuss

Pursue, search, and discuss the past,

옛 것을 구하여 찾고, 논의하며,

散	慮	逍	遙
산	려	소	요
흩어 버릴(동)	생각(명)	노닐(동)	거닐(동)
scatter	thought	stroll	walk

scatter thoughts, stroll, and walk.

잡념(생각)은 버리고 노닐며 걸어라.

744자
천자문(千字文)

欣	奏	累	遣
흔	주	누	견
기쁠(명)	아뢸(동)	곤란(명)	보낼(동)
delight	say	trouble	send

Say delight, send trouble,

기쁨은 아뢰고 곤란함은 보내며,

感	謝	歡	招
척	사	환	초
슬픔(명)	감사할(동)·사양할(동)	기쁠(명)	부를(동)
sadness	thank·decline	happiness	call

decline sadness, and call happiness.

슬픔은 보(사양)내고 기쁨은 불러라.

渠	荷	的	歷
거	하	적	력
개천(명)	연꽃(명)	과녁(동)·밝을(형용)	지낼(동)·분명할(형용)
ditch	lotus flower	target·bright	pass·clean

Lotus flowers are bright and clean in the ditch,

도랑의 연꽃들은 밝고 생기가 분명하며,

園	莽	抽	條
원	망	추	조
동산(명)	풀(명)	뽑을(동)·뻗을(동)	줄기(명)
garden	grass	pick·spread	stem

in the garden, grass spreads stems.

동산의 풀은 줄기들을 뻗고 있다.

枇	杷	晚	翠
비	파	만	취
비파나무(명)	비파나무(명)	늦을(부)	푸를(형용)
loquat	loquat	late	green

Loquat trees are green late,

비파나무는 늦게까지 푸르고,

梧	桐	早	凋
오	동	조	조
오동나무(명)	오동나무(동)	일찍(부)	시들(동)
paulownia	paulownia	early	wither

paulownia trees wither early.

오동나무는 일찍 시든다.

768자

천자문(千字文)

陳	根	委	翳
진	근	위	예
진칠(동)·늙은(형용)	뿌리(명)	쌓을(동)	마를(명)
encamp·old	root	pile	drought

Old roots piled up in drought,

늙은 뿌리는 말라 쌓이고,

落	葉	飄	颻
낙	엽	표	요
떨어질(동)	귤(명)	나부낄(동)	나부낄(동)
fall	leaf	flutter	flutter

fallen leaves flutter.

낙엽들은 나부낀다.

776자

천자문　　　　　　　　　　　　　　　　　　　　　　　　영어 풀이

遊	鯤	獨	運
유	곤	독	운
놀(동)	물고기(명)	홀로(부)	운전(동)
play	fish	alone	move

A Gon (fish) plays and moves alone,

곤(물고기)은 홀로 놀고 헤엄(운전)치며,

凌	摩	絳	霄
능	마	강	소
능가할(동)·무시할(동)	갈(동)·어루만질(동)	붉은(형용)	하늘(명)
excel·disregard	rub·pat	red	sky

pats the red sky, disregarding it.

붉은 하늘을 무시하며 즐긴다(어루만짐).

784자
천자문(千字文)

천자문   영어 풀이

耽	讀	翫	市
탐	독	완	시
즐길(동)	읽을(동)	놀(동)	시장(명)
enjoy	read	play	market

W. C. enjoyed reading, playing books in a market,

왕충은 시장에서 책과 놀고, 읽음을 즐겼고,

寓	目	囊	箱
우	목	낭	상
고정할(동)	눈(명)	주머니(명)	상자(명)
fix	eye	pocket	box

fixed eyes (reading books) into pockets, boxes.

눈(책을 읽는)을 주머니와 상자에 고정시켰다.

792자
천자문(千字文)

易	輶	攸	畏
이	유	유	외
쉬울(형용)	가벼울(형용)	바(명)	두려울(동)
easy	light	thing	fear

Fear easy and light things,

쉽고 가벼운 것을 두려워하라,

屬	耳	垣	墻
속	이	원	장
붙을(동)	귀(명)	담(명)	담(명)
have	ear	wall	wall

the wall has ears.

벽에도 귀가 있다.

800자
천자문(千字文)

具	膳	飡	飯
구	선	손	반
갖출(동)	반찬(명)	밥(명)	밥(명)
prepare	side dish	rice	rice

Prepare side dishes and rice,

반찬과 밥을 갖추고,

適	口	充	腸
적	구	충	장
맞을(동)	입(명)	충분할(동)	창자(명)
match	mouth	satisfy	bowel

match a mouth (eating) and satisfy bowels.

입(음식)을 맞추고 창자를 만족시킨다.

飽	飫	烹	宰
포	어	팽	재
배부를(형용)	배부를(형용)	삶을(동)	재상(명)·다스릴(동)
full	full	boil	premier·control

If full, boiled food is controlled,

배부르면 삶은 음식도 싫고(다스림),

飢	厭	糟	糠
기	염	조	강
배고플(형용)	싫을(형용)	찌꺼기(명)	겨(명)
hungry	bad	dreg	chaff

if hungry, dreg and chaff are not bad.

배가 고프면 찌꺼기와 겨도 싫지 않다.

親	戚	故	舊
친	척	고	구
친할(형용)	친척(명)	옛(형용)	옛(형용)·친구(명)
close	relative	old	old·friend

Relatives and old friends

친척과 옛 친구를

老	少	異	糧
노	소	이	량
늙을(명)	적을(명)	다를(동)	음식(명)
old	young	distinguish	food

distinguish for the old or young to foods.

나이 많고 적음에 따라 음식의 양을 다르게 하라.

妾	御	績	紡
첩	어	적	방
첩(명)	거느릴(동)	실 뽑을(동)	실 뽑을(동)
mistress	manage	spin	spin

A mistress spins, manages thread and,

첩(여자)은 실을 뽑고 다루며,

侍	巾	帷	房
시	건	유	방
모실(동)	수건(명)	장막(동)	방(명)
support	towel	curtain	room

supports with a towel in the curtained room.

장막 친 방에서 수건 들고 모신다.

紈	扇	圓	潔
환	선	원	결
하얀 비단(형용)	부채(명)	둥글(형용)	맑을(형용)
white silk	fan	round	clean

White silk fans are round and clean,

하얀 비단 부채들은 둥글고 맑으며,

銀	燭	煒	煌
은	촉	위	황
은(형용)	촛불(명)	빛날(동)	빛날(동)
silver	candlelight	shine	shine

silver candlelight shines.

은빛의 촛불이 빛난다.

840자

천자문(千字文)

천자문   영어 풀이

晝	眠	夕	寐
주	면	석	매
낮(명)	졸(동)	저녁(명)	잘(동)
day	doze	night	sleep

In the daytime, doze, at the night, sleep,

낮에 졸고 밤엔 잠을 잔다,

藍	筍	象	床
남	순	상	상
쪽빛(형용)	죽순(명)	코끼리(명)	상(명)
indigo	bamboo shoot	elephant	bed

on the bed with indigo bamboo shoot, elephants.

쪽빛의 죽순과 코끼리가 그려진 침대(상)에서.

848자

천자문(千字文)

絃	歌	酒	讌
현	가	주	연
줄(명)	노래(동)	술 마실(동)	잔치(명)
string	sing	wine	feast

Sing, play the strings, and wine in the feast,

잔치에서 거문고를 치고, 노래하고, 술을 마시며,

接	杯	擧	觴
접	배	거	상
접할(동)·잡을(동)	잔(명)	들(동)	잔(명)
join·hold	wine cup	raise	wine cup

hold and raise the wine cup.

술잔을 잡아 든다.

856자
천자문(千字文)

矯	手	頓	足
교	수	돈	족
바로잡을(동)·들(동)	손(명)	두드릴(동)	발(명)
correct·raise	hand	knock	foot

To raise hands and knock feet is,

손을 들고 발을 구르니,

說	豫	且	康
열	예	차	강
말씀(명)·기쁠(형용)	미리(부)·즐거울(형용)	또한(접속)	편할(형용)
word·pleasant	before·joyful	and	comfortable

pleasant, joyful, and comfortable.

기쁘고, 즐겁고, 또한 편안하다.

864자

천자문(千字文)

嫡	後	嗣	續
적	후	사	속
맏(명)	뒤(부)	이을(동)	이을(동)
firstborn son	after	succeed	succeed

The firstborn son succeeds, after,

맏아들이 나중에 대를 이으며,

祭	祀	蒸	嘗
제	사	증	상
제사(명)	제사 지낼(동)	찔(동)	맛볼(동)
ritual	perform	boil	taste

performs Jeong (ritual) and Sang (ritual).

증(제사)과 상(제사)을 지낸다.

稽	顙	再	拜
계	상	재	배
조아릴(동)	이마(명)	다시(부)	절(동)
bend	forehead	twice	bow

Bend a forehead and bow twice,

이마를 조아려 두 번(다시) 절한다,

悚	懼	恐	惶
송	구	공	황
미안할(부)	두려울(부)	두려울(부)	두려울(부)
sorrily	fearfully	fearfully	fearfully

sorrily and fearfully.

송구스럽고 두려워하며.

牋	牒	簡	要
전	첩	간	요
편지(명)	편지(명)	간략할(형용)	중요할(형용)
letter	letter	simple	important

A letter should be simple and important,

편지는 간략히 중요한 것만 있어야 하며,

顧	答	審	詳
고	답	심	상
돌아볼(동)	대답(동)	살필(동)	자세할(부)
consider	answer	observe	in detail

consider and observe in detail, when answering.

답변할 때 자세히 돌아보고 살펴라.

骸	垢	想	浴
해	구	상	욕
뼈(명)	더러울(형용)	생각(동)	목욕(명)
bone	dirty	think	bath

If a bone is dirty, think about a bath,

뼈가 더러워 지면, 목욕을 생각하고,

執	熱	願	涼
집	열	원	량
잡을(동)	뜨거울(명)	원할(동)	서늘할(명)
take	hotness	want	coolness

if taking hotness, want coolness.

뜨거운 것을 잡으면, 시원한 것을 원한다.

896자

천자문(千字文)

驢	騾	犢	特
려	라	독	특
나귀(명)	노새(명)	송아지(명)	황소(명)
donkey	mule	calf	cow

Donkeys, mules, calves, and cows

나귀, 노새, 송아지, 소들이

駭	躍	超	驤
해	약	초	양
놀랄(동)	뛸(동)	넘을(동)	달릴(동)
shock	run	jump	dash

shock, run, jump, and dash.

놀라고, 뛰고, 넘고, 그리고 달린다.

誅	斬	賊	盜
주	참	적	도
벨(동)	목 벨(동)	역적(명)	도둑(명)
kill	behead	rebel	thief

Kill and behead rebels and thieves,

역적과 도둑은 죽이고 참하며,

捕	獲	叛	亡
포	획	반	망
잡을(동)	잡을(동)	배반(동)	망할(동)·도망(동)
catch	catch	betray	ruin·escape

if betraying and escaping, catch.

배신하고 도망가면, 사로잡아라.

912자

천자문(千字文)

布	射	遼	丸
포	사	료	환
베(명)	쏠(동)	멀(형용)	공(명)
hemp cloth	shoot	far	ball

Yeo-po shot, Ung-ui-ryeo with a ball,

포(여포)는 화를 쐈고, 료(웅의료)는 공놀이를,

嵇	琴	阮	嘯
혜	금	완	소
메(명)	거문고(명)	성(명)	휘파람(동)
mountain	string	family name	whistle

Hye-gang with the strings, Wan-jeok whistled.

혜(혜강)은 거문고를, 완(완적)은 휘파람을 불었다.

恬	筆	倫	紙
염	필	륜	지
편안(형용)	붓(명)	인륜(명)	종이(명)
peaceful	brush	morality	paper

Mong-yeom's brush, Chae-ryun's paper,

염(몽염)의 붓, 륜(채륜)의 종이,

鈞	巧	任	釣
균	교	임	조
서른 근(명)	기교(명)	맡길(동)	낚시(명)
thirty	skill	keep	fishing

Ma-gyun's skills, Im-gong-ja's fishing (rod),

균(마균)의 기술, 임(임공자)의 낚시(대),

釋	紛	利	俗
석	분	이	속
풀(동)	어지러울(명)	좋을(형용)	세상(명)
solve	problem	good	world

they solved problems, made the world good,

앞의 모두는 세상의 어지러움을 풀고 좋고,

並	皆	佳	妙
병	개	가	묘
나란히(동)·하나하나(부)	모두(명)	아름다울(형용)	미묘할(형용)
row·one by one	all	beautiful	peculiar

one by one, all were beautiful and peculiar.

하나하나 모두가 아름답고 미묘하다.

毛	施	淑	姿
모	시	숙	자
털(명)	베풀(동)	맑을(형용)	모습(명)
hair	give	clean	appearance

Appearances of Mo-jang and Seo-si were clean,

모(모장)와 시(서시)의 모습은 맑았고,

工	嚬	妍	笑
공	빈	연	소
매혹할(동)	찡그릴(명)	고울(형용)	웃을(명)
fascinate	frown	beautiful	laugh

frown was fascinating, laugh was beautiful.

찡그림은 매혹적이고, 웃는 모습은 고왔다.

年	矢	每	催
년	시	매	최
해(명)·세월(명)	화살(명)	매일(부)	재촉할(동)
year	arrow	every day	fly

The year flies like an arrow every day,

세월은 화살처럼 매일 흘러(재촉) 가고,

羲	暉	朗	曜
희	휘	랑	요
사람이름(명)	빛(명)	빛날(동)	빛날(부)
Hui	sun	shine	brightly

the sun shines brightly.

태양은 밝게 빛난다.

952자
천자문(千字文)

천자문   영어 풀이

旋	璣	懸	斡
선	기	현	알
회전할(동)	돌(명)	매달(동)	회전할(동)
rotate	pearl	hang	rotate

Seon-gi (astronomical device) rotates hung,

선기(천문기구)는 매달려 돌고,

晦	魄	環	照
회	백	환	조
그믐달(명)	어두울(부)	고리(명)·순환할(동)	비칠(동)
old moon	darkly	ring·rotate	shine

the old moon shines rotating darkly.

그믐달은 돌(순환)면서 어둡게 빛난다.

960자
천자문(千字文)

指	薪	修	祐
지	신	수	우
손가락(동)	나무(명)	닦을(동)	복(명)
finger	wood	cultivate	fortune

If fingering wood and cultivating fortune,

나무에 손으로 불을 피고, 복을 닦으면,

永	綏	吉	邵
영	수	길	소
길(부)	평화(명)	길할(명)	높을(동)
long	peace	lucky	increase

peace and lucky increase long.

평화와 길함이 길게 높아질 것이다.

矩	步	引	領
구	보	인	령
규칙(부)	걸음(동)	당길(동)	옷깃(명)
regularly	walk	pull	collar

Walk regularly and pull the collar,

규칙적으로 걷고 옷깃을 바르게 하며(당기며),

俯	仰	廊	廟
부	앙	낭	묘
구부릴(부)	우러를(동)	행랑(명)	사당(명)
modestly	respect	room	government

respect Nang-myo (government) modestly.

겸손히(구부리면서) 낭묘(조정)을 우러러본다.

976자

束	帶	矜	莊
속	대	긍	장
묶을(동)	띠(명)	긍지(부)	엄할(부)
tie	belt	proudly	strictly

Tie a belt (waist) proudly and strictly,

긍지 있고 엄격하게 띠(허리)를 묶고,

徘	徊	瞻	眺
배	회	첨	조
배회할(동)	배회할(동)	볼(동)	볼(동)
wander	wander	look around	see

wandering, look around and see.

배회하면서 주위를 둘러본다.

984자

천자문(千字文)

孤	陋	寡	聞
고	루	과	문
외로울(형용)	추할(형용)	적을(명)	들을(동)
lonely	disgraceful	little	hear

To hear a little is disgraceful and lonely,

적게 배우는(들음)것은 외롭고 추하니,

愚	蒙	等	誚
우	몽	등	초
어리석을(형용)	어릴(형용)·우매할(형용)	무리(명)·같을(전치)	꾸짖을(동)
stupid	young·ignorant	crowd·like	scold

scold like the stupid and ignorant.

어리석고 우매한 사람처럼 꾸짖어라.

992자

천자문(千字文)

謂	語	助	者
위	어	조	자
이를(동)	말(명)	도울(동)	놈(명)·것(명)
say	word	help	person·thing

Things helping and saying words (particle) are

이야기와 말을 도와주는 것(어조사)은,

焉	哉	乎	也
언	재	호	야
어찌(부)·어조사	어조사	그런(감탄)·어조사	어조사
how·particle	particle	wow·particle	particle

⟨Eon · Jae · Ho · Ya⟩.

⟨언·재·호·야⟩ 이다.

English (천자문)

The Thousand Character Text

-영어 문장 밑에 부분에 뜻을 쓰시오-

보기

The Thousand Character Text
천 개의 글자로 이루어진 문장
written by Kim Master
김 선생님이 지은

천자문   영어 풀이

The sky is dark and the earth is yellow,

the world is wide and rough.

The sun goes down, the moon is filled,

stars spread and expand.

If the cold comes, the heat goes,

in autumn, harvest (foods), in winter, keep.

A leap month is made with extra days of a year,

Yin and Yang are balanced and harmonized.

If clouds go up, they become rains,

formed dew changes into frost.

Yeo-Su (Chinese village) produces gold,

Gon-Gang (Chinese mountain) produces jade.

Geo-gwol is a sword's name,

a bead (bright in the night) is called glow.

A plum and an apple are the best among fruits,

a mustard and a ginger are important herbs.

Sea (water) is salty and river (water) is fresh,

fish (scales) are under water, birds (wings) fly.

A office with a dragon (B·H) and fire (Y·J),

an office with a bird (S·H) and (H·W) is humanity.

First, Chang-hil (Bok-hui's servant) made a letter,

besides, people wore clothes to know status.

Je-yo conceded his state to Je-sun,

Yu-u (J·S) and Do-dang (J·Y) were emperors.

Help poor people, punish the faulty,

Ju-bal, Eun-tang are names of Ju and Tang king.

Sitting in the Royal Palace, ask the way,

dropping and folding arms is peaceful and bright.

If raising people having black hairs with love,

barbarians (Yung and Gang) obey like servants.

Countries far and near will be one body,

lead guests, and come back to the king.

A phoenix is on the tree, crying,

a white colt will eat meal on the ground.

Harmony spread to grass and trees,

trust will reach to all the place.

Hairs cover this body,

there are four greatnesses and five constancies.

Be only polite about raising you,

how dare you injury and hurt (your body)?

Women yearn for courtesy firmly,

men follow skill and good.

If knowing a fault, correct necessarily,

if getting ability, don't forget.

Don't say a defect of others,

don't rely on merit of yourself.

Don't make trust change well,

wanting to know a bowl (ability) is difficult.

Muk-ja was sad about thread being dyed,

《Poetry》 praised men wearing goat clothes.

If doing the great basis, you will be wise,

if overcoming thoughts, you will make a sage.

To build virtue is to make your name,

if a face is right, appearance will be right.

An empty valley's sound spreads,

an empty room's sound is heard and practiced.

To build badness causes misfortune,

goodness and happiness cause fortune.

A small bead can't be a treasure,

a moment should be competed (not the bead).

Basing the father, serve the king,

say to the king strictly and politely.

Do your best to try filial piety naturally,

when in loyalty, that is, devote your life.

On shallows, walk like facing on deeps,

rise early, and keep (parent) warm and cool.

Like an orchid, keep that scent,

like a pine, flourish.

A running stream doesn't break,

a clean pond has the reflection.

Show and behave like thinking,

say words comfortably and easily.

천자문 영어 풀이

First, do diligently, sincerely, and mannerly,

make an end carefully, naturally,

that (289~296 words) is basic to develop work,

(your) name will be well without ending.

If learning much, you can climb office,

holding office, follow politics.

So-gong was at a sweet hawthorn,

left, but the people recited a more poem for him.

The elegance has high and low differently,

manners distinguishes the upper from lower.

If a senior is peaceful, a junior is peaceful,

if a husband guides, a wife follows.

천자문   영어 풀이

In outside, receive a lesson from a teacher,

if coming (house), follow a mother's behavior.

All aunt, elder uncle, and younger uncle should

think of other kids as their children.

Brothers should get along well,

as they stem from the same branch and spirit.

Associate with friends giving the status,

practice justice earnestly and carefully.

Virtue, mercy, compassion, and pity

don't leave for even a moment.

Fidelity, justice, integrity, and retreat

don't weaken, if collapsing and falling.

If nature is calm, feeling is comfortable,

if mind shakes, spirit is fatigue.

If keeping the truth, the will is filled,

if pursuing property, meaning changes.

If having the right principle firmly,

likable office happens naturally.

Hwa-ha (China) made towns and villages,

in the east and west are two capitals.

Mt. Buk is at the back, Nak water is at the front,

Wi water floats and base on Gyeong water.

As there are many palaces,

on upstairs, if looking at, you will fly, surprised.

천자문   영어 풀이

Drawing birds and animals in a painting,

color hermits and spirits in the painting.

Next to Byeong-sa (building), open the door,

Gap-jang (colorful curtains) sits opposite pillars.

Placing a mat and making a seat,

drum the harp and play the flute.

Going up stairs, enter stone steps,

hats (ornaments) waving, doubt stars.

On the right, pass Gwang-nae (building),

on the left, pass Seung-myeong (building).

Collect, ahead, Bun (book) and Jeon (book),

also, gather many talents.

Du-go's grass characters, Jong-yo's angular styles,

lacquered books and bibles are in the wall.

In the office, generals stand together,

three dukes and officers are on the road together.

As a house, Han state gave eight counties,

gave a thousand soldiers to the house.

High hats (high officer) serve a wagon,

turning wheels, hat strings wave.

For the generation, with pay, luxury, wealth,

fat (horse) draw light wagons and vehicles.

Planning merits and increasing results,

engrave a name on a tombstone.

Ban-gye (Gang-tae-gong) and I-yun (A-hyeong),

are helpers (found of Ju and Eun state).

Cover Gok-bu (area)'s house,

who manages it in detail? Dan (Ju-gong).

Hwan duke unified uprightly,

relieved the weak, and helped the decline (state).

Gi-ri-gye replaced Hye-je of Han state,

Bu-yeol impressed Mu-jeong (King of Sang state).

Surely, the high good and virtue,

many scholars, this is peaceful.

Jin (Mun duke), Cho (Jang king) changed a chief,

Jo and Wi had difficulty for Heong (strategy).

천자문   영어 풀이

After renting a way from Goek, to ruin Goek,

gathering in Cheon-to (place), to swear.

So-ha followed the simple law,

Han-bi-ja had hardship for the complex law.

Baek-gi, Wang-jeon, Yeom-pa, and I-mok

used soldiers extremely and finely,

spread dignity to the desert,

honor ran with Dan-cheong (picture).

Nine villages are King U's trace,

Jin state managed one-hundred districts.

Hang and Dae are best big mountains,

Un and Jeong are mains (place) of a hermit (rite).

An-mun, Ja-sae,

Gye-jeon, Jeok-seong (place),

Gon-ji (lake), Gal-seok (mountain),

Geo-ya (swamp), Dong-jeong (lake)

connect in the distance and far away,

rocks and mountain peaks are away and subtly.

Basically, govern with agriculture,

further, try to plant and harvest.

Finally, fill furrows in the south,

I plant millet and grass.

Tax the ripe, offer the new,

advise, prize, send, and promote it.

Maeng-ga (Maeng-ja) strengthened basis,

Sa-eo (a minister of Wi state) had honesty.

To approach Jung-Yong (the golden mean),

work hard, be modest, cautious, and alert.

hearing the sound, observe the reason,

seeing appearance, recognize the face.

Hand down the good plan,

try to keep it politely.

Observe, reflect, and watch out for your body,

if gaining favor, dispute the end.

If dishonor is dangerous and close to disgrace,

soon, in the forest and hill, be happy.

천자문　　　　　　　　　　　　　　　　　　　　영어 풀이

As two So (So-gwang and So-su) saw a condition,

they untied strings, who pressured them?

Search the free place, and live,

sinking, silently, quietly, and solitarily.

Pursue, search, and discuss the past,

scatter thoughts, stroll, and walk.

Say delight, send trouble,

decline sadness, and call happiness.

Lotus flowers are bright and clean in the ditch,

in the garden, grass spreads stems.

Loquat trees are green late,

paulownia trees wither early.

천자문   영어 풀이

Old roots piled up in drought,

fallen leaves flutter.

A Gon (fish) plays and moves alone,

pats the red sky, disregarding it.

W. C. enjoyed reading, playing books in a market,

fixed eyes (reading books) into pockets, boxes.

Fear easy and light things,

the wall has ears.

Prepare side dishes and rice,

match a mouth (eating) and satisfy bowels.

If full, boiled food is controlled,

if hungry, dreg and chaff are not bad.

Relatives and old friends

distinguish for the old or young to foods.

A mistress (woman) spins, manages thread and,

supports with a towel in the curtained room.

White silk fans are round and clean,

silver candlelight shines.

In the daytime, doze, at the night, sleep,

on the bed with indigo bamboo shoot, elephants.

Sing, play the strings, and wine in the feast,

hold and raise the wine cup.

To raise hands and knock feet is,

pleasant, joyful, and comfortable.

The firstborn son succeeds, after,

performs Jeong (ritual) and Sang (ritual).

Bend a forehead and bow twice,

sorrily and fearfully.

A letter should be simple and important,

consider and observe in detail, when answering.

If a bone becomes dirty, think about a bath,

if taking hotness, want coolness.

Donkeys, mules, calves, and cows

shock, run, jump, and dash.

Kill and behead rebels and thieves,

if betraying and escaping, catch.

천자문　　　　　　　　　　　　　　　　　　　　영어 풀이

Yeo-po shot, Ung-ui-ryeo with a ball,

Hye-gang with the strings, Wan-jeok whistled.

Mong-yeom's brush, Chae-ryun's paper,

Ma-gyun's skills, Im-gong-ja's fishing (rod),

they solved problems, made the world good,

one by one, all were beautiful and peculiar.

Appearances of Mo-jang and Seo-si were clean,

frown was fascinating, laugh was beautiful.

The year flies like an arrow every day,

the sun shines brightly.

Seon-gi (astronomical device) rotates hung,

the old moon shines rotating darkly.

If fingering wood and cultivating fortune,

peace and lucky increase long.

Walk regularly and pull the collar,

respect Nang-myo (government) modestly.

Tie a belt (waist) proudly and strictly,

wandering, look around and see.

To hear a little is disgraceful and lonely,

scold like the stupid and ignorant.

Things helping and saying words (particle) are

⟨Eon · Jae · Ho · Ya⟩.

English (사자소학)

The Four Characters Small Learning

-영어 문장 밑에 부분에 뜻을 쓰시오-

보기

The Four Character Small Learning
네 글자의 작은 학문
written by Kim Master
김 선생님이 지은

A father produced me,

a mother raised my body.

With a belly, she embraced me,

with milk, she fed me.

With clothes, they kept me warm,

With foods, they kept me lively,

the blessing is high like the sky,

the virtue is deep like the earth.

As a child of people,

why couldn't we do filial piety?

If you want to repay their deep benefits,

it is like the endless big sky.

If parents call me,

just, say "yes" and run forward.

The order of parents

don't disobey and be lazy to it.

When you support parents before them,

don't sit astride and lie.

To meet a table and not to eat is

to think about getting good dishes.

If parents are sick,

plan to cure them carefully.

If parents send rice and food,

don't be lazy to reading a book.

천자문   영어 풀이

Parents' saliva and phlegm

always, bury necessarily.

If telling them you go to the west,

don't go to the east.

When going outside, tell parents it necessarily,

when coming back, say it to them necessarily.

When standing, see their foot soon,

when sitting, see their knee soon.

At evening, settle the bedding necessarily,

at dawn, observe parents' conditions necessarily.

If parents love me,

be delight, not forget it.

천자문 / 영어 풀이

Though parents hate me,

don't fear or blame it.

Don't walk arrogantly,

when sitting, don't lean back.

Don't stand in the middle of the door,

don't sit in the middle of the room.

When a chicken cries, wake up,

wash hands and brush teeth necessarily.

Take care of saying words necessarily,

live in a place politely necessarily.

Frist, when you learn a text and a word,

write and follow words correctly.

The age of parents

you must know naturally.

Though foods or drinks are bad,

if parents give them, you should eat them.

Though clothes are bad,

if parents give them, you should wear them.

Clothes, a belt, and shoes

you should not lose and tear.

Though the coldness comes, endure it,

in the heat, don't roll up pants or a skirt.

In summer, soon, fan next to parents" pillow,

in winter, soon, warm their blanket.

When supporting parents next to them,

go forward and back politely.

Don't sit before parents' knee,

don't look up at their face.

Though parents order, lying,

bend your head and listen.

A living place should be comfortable and quiet,

when walking, you should be easy and clear.

Eating fully, wearing warmly,

without lesson, and living enjoying is,

that is, closely related to birds and animals,

a sage worries.

To love parents and to respect elder brother is

good knowledge and ability.

Don't use a mouth to say useless stories,

don't use hands to play useless things.

When sleeping soon, tie blankets,

eat soon on the same table together.

If you borrow a book from someone,

don't damage with perfection.

If an elder brother has no clothes,

a little brother should offer clothes.

If a little brother has no drink and food,

an elder brother should give necessarily.

When your elder brother is hungry, if you are full,

you are doing like birds and animals.

A feeling of brothers is

in loving and valuing with fraternity.

When eating foods before parents,

don't make sound of bowls.

Live choosing neighbors necessarily,

when entering something, be with the virtue.

Parents' clothes

don't go over and step on.

A table and an ink-stone used to write

should be faced with that bottom rightly.

Don't fight with other people,

as parents worry.

When coming out, entering the door of a house,

open and close the door politely.

Paper, a brush, a ink-stone, and ink

we call the four precious things of the study.

By day, cultivate a field, by night, read a book,

in summer, study manners, in spring, poems.

If words are different from deeds mutually,

disgrace will reach your ancestors.

If deeds are not like your words,

disgrace will reach your body.

Support parents with extreme filial piety,

support parents' will and whole body well.

To seek a bamboo shoot in the snow is

filial piety of Maeng-Jong (person's name).

To break ice and to get a carp is

filial piety of Wang-Sang (person's name).

At dawn, wake up earlier than parents necessarily,

at sunset, sleep later than parents naturally.

In winter be warm, in summer be cool,

in evening make a bed, in dawn observe parents.

When you come out, don't change a place,

when playing, have a place necessarily.

Your whole body, hair, and skin are

received from parents,

not dare to hurt them is

the first of filial piety.

To stand your body and do the way,

to make your name after in world,

to show your parents' name is

the last of filial piety.

Word should be loyal and trustworthy,

deeds should be honest and upright necessarily.

If you see the good, you should follow it,

if you know a fault, you should correct it.

A face and appearance should be right and strict,

arrange clothes and a hat strictly.

When starting a task, first, you should plan well,

when starting speaking, observe deeds.

You should always hold the firm virtue,

and, replying, respond prudently.

Food and drink should be controlled prudently,

words should be done politely and mildly.

To wake up, live, sit, and stand is

your deed and movement.

Manners, justice, upright, and shame

we call it the four natures.

천자문   영어 풀이

Advise the virtuous work mutually,

correct faults and errors mutually,

associate with people with politeness mutually,

help people facing anxiety and difficulty mutually.

A father should be right and a mother merciful,

an elder brother friendly, a little brother polite.

A husband and a wife should have favor,

man and woman should have their difference.

Poverty, difficulty, anxiety, and difficulty

close relatives should help mutually.

Marriage and the time of mourning

neighbors should protect and help mutually.

Being in a house, a woman follows her father,

after marriage, a woman follows her husband,

after husband's death, a woman follows a son,

we call it three ways (three followings).

Won-Hyung-Li-Jung (four virtues in 《Ju Yeok》) is

fairness of Heaven's way.

Mercy, justice, manners, and wisdom are

basis of a person' nature.

If it is not manners, don't look at,

if it is not manners, don't hear,

if it is not manners, don't speak,

if it is not manners, don't move,

The way of Confucian and Mencius,

the learning of Jung brothers and Chu-Shi are

to right this justice,

they don't plan that profit,

they illuminate that way,

they don't count that merits,

though declining a road,

they would not bend a hundred walking,

though declining a ridge,

they would not lose one part at all.

The sky opens at the hour of the Rat,

the earth opens at the hour of the Cow.

People were born at the hour of the Tiger,

we call it ancient times.

A king should do the basis of subjects,

a father should do the basis of children,

a husband should do the basis of a wife,

we call it the three basic principles.

Parents and children should have familiarity,

a king and subjects should have justice.

a husband and a wife should have difference,

the old and the young should have order,

fellows and friends should have trust,

we call it the five principles of morality.

Looking at something, necessarily, think it clearly,

hearing something, necessarily, think it cleverly,

think your face's color is warm necessarily,

think your appearance is polite necessarily,

speaking, think it is loyal necessarily,

working, think you can avoid it necessarily,

when doubting, ask it necessarily.

angering, think about the difficulty necessarily,

looking at gains, necessarily, think it is right,

we call it the nice thoughts.

An aspect of foots should be heavy necessarily,

an aspect of hands should be polite necessarily,

an aspect of eyes should be right necessarily,

an aspect of a mouth should be closed,

an aspect of a voice should be clam necessarily,

an aspect of breath should be strict necessarily,

an aspect of a head should be right necessarily,

a standing aspect should be virtuous necessarily,

color of your face should be lively necessarily,

we call it the nine aspects.

To cultivate a body and to govern a house is

the foundation of governing a nation.

A scholar, a farmer, a craftsman, and a merchant

give a nation the benefits.

A widower, a widow, an orphan, and the elderly

we call the four poverties,

when starting to govern or giving the true virtue,

first, give it to the four people.

In a village having ten houses,

there are loyal and trustworthy people.

Originally, this filial-piety thing

the foundation of practicing the true virtue.

Words should be trusty and true,

behave deeply and politely necessarily.

Though there is one grain of cereals,

share and eat necessarily,

though there is one suit,

share and wear necessarily.

If a house saves the good,

there will be extra congratulations necessarily,

if a house saves the bad,

there will be extra disasters necessarily.

My word is not the word of the old,

only, the plan of the sage.

Alas! Alas! Young children!

Receive this book politely.

As a person having read this book,

why couldn't you do filial piety without enduring!

Table of Consanguinity
촌수법(寸數法)

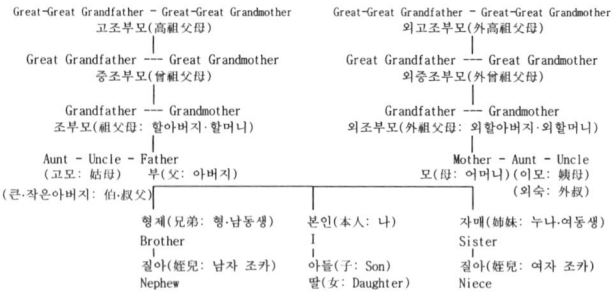

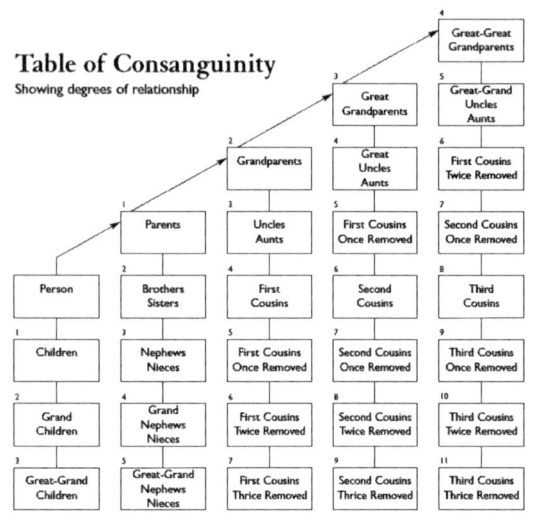